QUOTES FROM FAMOUS PERSONALITIES

I0428498

FROM THE PAST TO THE PRESENT: POLITICANS TO POP STARS

SUSHEEL LADWA

Author of *10,001 Quotes & Sayings*

ISBN: 1503385019
ISBN-13: 978-1503385016

Mamata and Vishwanath Ladwa

My Mother and Father

"All I Am, I Owe To You"

ACKNOWLEDGMENTS

Writing a book starts as a hobby, becomes a passion, and rules your dreams until it becomes a reality. I gave it time because it is my passion. I want to acknowledge the people that gave their time and support to help realize my passion.

I wanted to thank my wife, Preetha, for her patience, love and support through the blur of day and night with a month old baby. This book would not have been possible without her. Every time there is a knock on my office door, there enters a big beautiful smile that makes it all worth it – Ruhi, my daughter, my friend, my little philosopher and guide. The new bundle of joy of the family – Syon, he is a month old but has shown who the boss is.

My brother, Sunil, my sister-in-law, Sumitra, and kids, Shreya, Kushi, and Arya, for their love and faith in me.

Last but not the least, my editor Jesse Kimmel-Freeman, for all the cattle she chased while editing my book – Thank you!

We are living in a world, where what we earn is a function of what we learn. - Bill Clinton

Your most unhappy customers are your greatest source of learning. - Bill Gates

You put water into a cup, it becomes the cup. You put water into a teapot, it becomes the teapot. Now water can crash, drip, flow ... be water my friend. - Bruce Lee

You will not be punished for your anger; you will be punished by your anger. – Buddha

Nothing before had ever made me thoroughly realise, though I had read various scientific books, that science consists in grouping facts so that general laws or conclusions may be drawn from them. - Charles Darwin

Perpetual optimism is a force multiplier. - Colin Powell

Share your knowledge. It's a way to achieve immortality. - Dalai Lama

The future belongs to those who believe in the beauty of their dreams. - Eleanor Roosevelt

The time to repair the roof is when the sun is shining. - John F. Kennedy

Vote early and vote often. - Al Capone

The only way to do great work is to love what you do. If you haven't found it yet, keep looking. Don't settle. - Steve Jobs

We are just an advanced breed of monkeys on a minor planet of a very average star. But we can understand the Universe. That makes us something very special. - Stephen Hawking

Dance like nobody's watching; love like you've never been hurt. Sing like nobody's listening; live like it's heaven on earth. - Mark Twain

You must be the change you wish to see in the world. - Mahatma Gandhi

Love is needing to be loved. - John Lennon

Your children need your presence more than your presents. - Jesse Jackson

Bad news isn't wine. It doesn't improve with age. - Colin Powell

Willing is not enough; we must do. Knowing is not enough; we must apply. - Bruce Lee

As we look ahead into the next century, leaders will be those who empower others. - Bill Gates

Never pick a fight with people who buy ink by the barrel. - Bill Clinton

A film has its own life and takes its own time. - Aaron Eckhart

Always be nice to your children because they are the ones who will choose your rest home. - Phyllis Diller

As the family goes, so goes the nation and so goes

the whole world in which we live. - Pope John Paul II

Bitterness is like cancer. It eats upon the host. But anger is like fire. It burns it all clean. - Maya Angelou

Children have never been very good at listening to their elders, but they have never failed to imitate them. - James Baldwin

Courage is being scared to death but saddling up anyway. - John Wayne

———◆———

Every great film should seem new every time you
see it. - Roger Ebert

———◆———

Happiness is having a large, loving, caring, close-
knit family in another city. - George Burns

———◆———

Ignorance more frequently begets confidence than
does knowledge: it is those who know little, and not
those who know much, who so positively assert that
this or that problem will never be solved by science.
- Charles Darwin

———◆———

In order to succeed, your desire for success should be greater than your fear of failure. - Bill Cosby

It is not the strongest of the species that survive, nor the most intelligent, but the one most responsive to change. - Charles Darwin

It is very important to generate a good attitude, a good heart, as much as possible. From this, happiness in both the short term and the long term for both yourself and others will come. - Dalai Lama

It takes courage to grow up and turn out to be who you really are. - E.E. Cummings

---

Life is tough, and if you have the ability to laugh at it you have the ability to enjoy it. - Salma Hayek

---

Love is like a virus. It can happen to anybody at any time. - Maya Angelou

---

Mistakes are always forgivable, if one has the courage to admit them. - Bruce Lee

Money won't create success. The freedom to make it will. - Nelson Mandela

Movies can and do have tremendous influence in shaping young lives in the realm of entertainment towards the ideals and objectives of normal adulthood. - Walt Disney

Music in the soul can be heard by the universe. - Lao Tzu

Music is a safe kind of high. - Jimi Hendrix

Nobody can give you freedom. Nobody can give

you equality or justice or anything. If you're a man, you take it. - Malcolm X

Peace cannot be kept by force; it can only be achieved by understanding. - Albert Einstein

Success is liking yourself, liking what you do, and liking how you do it. - Maya Angelou

The average Hollywood film stars ambition is to be admired by an American, courted by an Italian, married to an Englishman, and have a French boyfriend. - Katharine Hepburn

The best jokes are dangerous, and dangerous because they are in some way truthful. - Kurt Vonnegut

The best reason to make a film is that you feel passionately about it. - Jodie Foster

The greatest discovery of all time is that a person can change his future by merely changing his attitude. - Oprah Winfrey

The saddest aspect of life right now is that science gathers knowledge faster than society gathers wisdom. - Isaac Asimov

The secret to staying young is to live honestly, eat slowly, and lie about your age. - Lucille Ball

The way to get started is to quit talking and begin doing. - Walt Disney

This film cost $31 million. With that kind of money I could have invaded some country. - Clint Eastwood

Women don't want to hear what you think. Women want to hear what they think in a deeper voice. - Bill Cosby

Women marry men hoping they will change. Men marry women hoping they will not. So each is inevitably disappointed. - Albert Einstein

You are not special. You are not a beautiful or unique snowflake. You are the same decaying organic matter as everything else. - Chuck Palahniuk

You must be the change you wish to see in the world. – Gandhi

---

A day without laughter is a day wasted. - Charlie Chaplin

A friendship founded on business is a good deal better than a business founded on friendship. - John D Rockerfeller

---

A lie cannot live. - Martin Luther King Jr.

A lot of places can be the wrong place at the wrong time. - Bill Clinton

A man has one hundred dollars and you leave him with two dollars, that's subtraction. - Mae West

A man in love is incomplete until he has married. Then he's finished. - Zsa Zsa Gabor

A man must be willing to die for justice. Death is an inescapable reality and men die daily, but good deeds live forever. - Jesse Jackson

A man will fight harder for his interests than for his rights. - Napoleon Bonaparte

A scientific man ought to have no wishes, no affections, -- a mere heart of stone. -Charles Darwin

A word to the wise ain't necessary -- it's the stupid ones that need the advice. - Bill Cosby

Acting is the expression of a neurotic impulse? It's a bum's life. The principal benefit acting has afforded

me is the money to pay for my psychoanalysis. -
Marlon Brando

Advertising is the most fun you can have with your
clothes on. - Bill Cosby

Airplane travel is nature's way of making you look
like your passport photo. - Al Gore

All enterprises that are entered into with indiscreet
zeal may be pursued with great vigor at first, but
are sure to collapse in the end. – Tacitus

All our dreams can come true --if we have the courage to pursue them. - Walt Disney

All our knowledge has its origin in our perceptions. - Leonardo da Vinci

All praise is to Allah, I'll fight any man, any animal, if Jesus were here I'd fight him too. - Mike Tyson

All that is gold does not glitter; not all those that wander are lost. - J.R.R. Tolkien

All the people throughout my life who were naysayers pissed me off. But they've all given me a fervor; an angry ambition that cannot be stopped - and I look forward to finding a therapist and working on that. - Tobey Maguire

Always be on time. Do as little talking as humanly possible. Remember to lean back in the parade so everybody can see the president. Be sure not to get too fat, because you'll have to sit three in the back. - Eleanor Roosevelt

Always remember, others may hate you- but those who hate you don't win unless you hate them, and then you destroy yourself. - Richard Nixon

America did not invent human rights. In a very real sense ... human rights invented America. - Jimmy Carter

America will never seek a permission slip to defend the security of our people. - George W. Bush

An actor is at most a poet and at least an entertainer. - Marlon Brando

An actor's a guy, who if you ain't talking about him, ain't listening. - Marlon Brando

An education isn't how much you have committed to memory, or even how much you know. It's being able to differentiate between what you know and what you don't. - Malcolm Forbes

Any fool can make things bigger, more complex, and more violent. It takes a touch of genius -- and a lot of courage -- to move in the opposite direction. - Albert Einstein

Anyone can dabble, but once you've made that commitment, your blood has that particular thing in it, and it's very hard for people to stop you. - Bill Cosby

Anyone can get old, all you have to do is live long enough. - Groucho Marx

Anything worth doing is worth doing slowly. - Mae West

Art calls for complete mastery of techniques, developed by reflection within the soul. - Bruce Lee

As a matter of principle, I never attend the first annual anything. - George Carlin

As a rule, men worry more about what they can't see than about what they can. - Julius Caesar

As a woman, I find it very embarrassing to be in a meeting and realize I'm the only one in the room with balls. - Rita Mae Brown

As far as I am concerned now, I have no enemies in the press whatsoever. - Richard Nixon

As long as you're going to be thinking anyway,

think big. - Donald Trump

Bad artists copy. Great artists steal. - Pablo Picasso

Be who you are and say what you feel, because those who mind don't matter and those who matter don't mind. - Theodor Seuss Geisel

Beauty is a sign of intelligence. - Andy Warhol

Behind every successful man is a woman, behind her is his wife. - Groucho Marx

Being able to touch so many people through my businesses and make money while doing it, is a huge blessing. - Magic Johnson

Being responsible sometimes means pissing people off. - Colin Powell

Better to live one year as a tiger, then a hundred as sheep. - Madonna Ciccone

By our efforts, we have lit a fire as well -- a fire in the minds of men. It warms those who feel its power, it burns those who fight its progress, and one day this untamed fire of freedom will reach the darkest corners of our world. - George W. Bush

Capital punishment turns the state into a murderer, but imprisonment turns the state into a gay dungeon-master. - Jesse Jackson

Carpe per diem - seize the check. - Robin Williams

Chance favors the prepared mind. - Louis Pasteur

Chaos in the midst of chaos isn't funny, but chaos in the midst of order is. - Steve Martin

Children today know more about sex than I or my father did. - Bill Cosby

Christmas can be celebrated in the school room with pine trees, tinsel and reindeers, but there must be no mention of the man whose birthday is being celebrated. One wonders how a teacher would answer if a student asked why it was called Christmas. - Ronald Reagan

Christmas is a time when everybody wants his past forgotten and his present remembered. - Phyllis Diller

Christmas is the one time of year when people of all religions come together to worship Santa Claus. - Bart Simpson

Cocaine is God's way of telling someone that they're too rich. - Robin Williams

Comedy is the art of making people laugh without making them puke. - Steve Martin

Courage is being scared to death, but saddling up anyway. - John Wayne

Courage is the first of human qualities because it is the quality which guarantees all others. - Winston Churchill

Democracy means that anyone can grow up to be president, and anyone who doesn't grow up can be vice president. - Johnny Carson

Do what you feel in your heart to be right- for you'll be criticized anyway. You'll be damned if you do, and damned if you don't. - Eleanor Roosevelt

Do, or do not. There is no 'try.' - Jedi Master Yoda

Dogs look up to you. Cats look down on you. Pigs treat you like equals. - Winston Churchill

Don't cry because it's over. Smile because it happened. - Theodor Seuss Geisel

---

Don't knock masturbation; it's sex with someone I love. - Woody Allen

Don't marry a man to reform him - that's what reform schools are for. - Mae West

---

Don't worry about the world coming to an end today. It's already tomorrow in Australia. - Charles Schulz

Drama is life with the dull bits cut out. - Alfred

Hitchcock

Dying is the most embarrassing thing that can ever happen to you, because someone's got to take care of all your details. - Andy Warhol

Education's purpose is to replace an empty mind with an open one. - Malcolm Forbes

Effective leadership is putting first things first. Effective management is discipline, carrying it out. - Stephen Covey

English? Who needs that? I'm never going to England. - Homer Simpson

Ernest Hemingway once wrote, 'The world is a fine place and worth fighting for.' I agree with the second part. - Morgan Freeman

Even if there is only one possible unified theory, it is just a set of rules and equations. What is it that breathes fire into the equations and makes a universe for them to describe? - Stephen Hawking

Ever notice that 'what the hell' is always the right decision? - Marilyn Monroe

Every act of creation is first of all an act of destruction. - Pablo Picasso

Everything in the world may be endured except continued prosperity. - Johann Wolfgang von Goethe

Everything that used to be a sin is now a disease. - Bill Maher

Everything you can imagine is real. - Pablo Picasso

Experience is the teacher of all things. - Julius Caesar

Extraordinary claims require extraordinary proof. - Carl Sagan

Fantasy is a necessary ingredient in living, it's a way of looking at life through the wrong end of a telescope and that enables you to laugh at life's realities. - Theodor Seuss Geisel

Far and away the best prize that life offers is the chance to work hard at work worth doing. - Theodore Roosevelt

Fatherhood is pretending the present you love most is soap on-a-rope. - Bill Cosby

Feminism was established to allow unattractive women easier access to the mainstream. - Rush Limbaugh

Few men have virtue to withstand the highest bidder. - George Washington

Fiction is the truth inside the lie. - Stephen King

Find me a man who's interesting enough to have dinner with and I'll be happy. - Lauren Bacall

First the doctor told me the good news: I was going to have a disease named after me. - Steve Martin

First they ignore you, then they ridicule you, then they fight you, then you win. - Mahatma Gandhi

---

First think, second believe, third dream and finally dare. - Walt Disney

---

For all of its faults, it gives most hardworking people a chance to improve themselves economically, even as the deck is stacked in favor of the privileged few. Here are the choices most of us face in such a system: Get bitter or get busy. - Bill O Reilly

---

For three days after death, hair and fingernails continue to grow but phone calls taper off. - Johnny

Carson

For two people in a marriage to live together day after day is unquestionably the one miracle the Vatican has overlooked. - Bill Cosby

Forever is composed of nows. - Emily Dickinson

Forgiveness is not an occasional act: it is a permanent attitude. - Martin Luther King Jr.

Freedom and fear, justice and cruelty, have always been at war, and we know that God is not neutral between them. - George W. Bush

Freedom is the right to question and change the established way of doing things. It is the continuous revolution of the marketplace. It is the understanding that allows us to recognize shortcomings and seek solutions. - Ronald Reagan

Friendship with oneself is all-important because without it one cannot be friends with anyone else in the world. - Eleanor Roosevelt

Frisbeetarianism is the belief that when you die,

your soul goes up on the roof and gets stuck. -
George Carlin

From kindergarten to graduation, I went to public
schools, and I know that they are a key to being sure
that every child has a chance to succeed and to rise
in the world. - Dick Cheney

From the moment I picked your book up until I laid
it down I was convulsed with laughter. Some day I
intend reading it. - Groucho Marx

Genius is personality with two measures of talent. -
Pablo Picasso

Get happiness out of your work or you may never know what happiness is. - Elbert Hubbard

Get your facts first, then you can distort them as you please. - Mark Twain

Getting divorced just because you don't love a man is almost as silly as getting married just because you do. - Zsa Zsa Gabor

Give a man a free hand and he'll run it all over you.

- Mae West

God does not play dice with the universe. - Albert Einstein

God is a concept by which we measure our pain. - John Lennon

God is really only another artist. He invented the giraffe, the elephant and the cat. He has no real style, He just goes on trying other things. - Pablo Picasso

Goldie and I did have a car stolen right out of our yard. It took us three days to notice. - Kurt Russell

Good sex is like good Bridge: if you don't have a good partner, you'd better have a good hand. – Mae West

Great leaders are almost always great simplifiers, who can cut through argument, debate, and doubt to offer a solution everybody can understand. - Colin Powell

Happiness in intelligent people is the rarest thing I know. - Ernest Hemingway

Happiness is a butterfly, which, when pursued, is always just beyond your grasp, but which, if you will sit down quietly, may alight upon you. - Nathaniel Hawthorne

Happiness is having a large, loving, caring, close-knit family in another city. - George Burns

Hate cannot drive out hate; only love can do that. - Martin Luther King Jr.

Have you ever noticed that anybody driving slower than you is an idiot, and anyone going faster than you is a maniac? - George Carlin

Hope for the Best. Expect the worst. Life is a play. We're unrehearsed. - Mel Brooks

How did it get so late so soon? It's night before it's afternoon. December is here before it's June. My goodness how the time has flown. How did it get so late so soon? - Theodor Seuss Geisel

How do you tell a Communist? Well, it's someone who reads Marx and Lenin. And how do you tell an anti-Communist? It's someone who understands Marx and Lenin. - Ronald Reagan

How lucky for those in power that people don't think. - Adolf Hitler

I am a little pencil in the hand of a writing God who is sending a love letter to the world. - Mother Teresa

I am always doing that which I cannot do, in order that I may learn how to do it. - Pablo Picasso

I am certainly not an authority on love because there are no authorities on love, just those who've had luck with it and those who haven't. - Bill Cosby

I am not a has-been. I am a will be. - Lauren Bacall

I am the literary equivalent of a Big Mac and Fries. - Stephen King

I believe that sex is one of the most beautiful, natural, wholesome things that money can buy. -

Steve Martin

I can live for two months on a good compliment. - Mark Twain

I can sell out Madison Square Garden masturbating. - Mike Tyson

I can't think of a better way to spread the message of world peace than by working with the NFL and being part of Super Bowl XXVII.- Michael Jackson

---

I cordially dislike allegory in all its manifestations, and always have done since I grew old and wary enough to detect its presence. - J.R.R. Tolkien

I could not handle being a woman, I would stay home all day and play with my breasts. - Steve Martin

I don't get acting jobs because of my looks. - Alec Baldwin

I don't know half of you half as well as I should like; and I like less than half of you half as well as you deserve. - J.R.R. Tolkien

I don't know the key to success, but the key to failure is to try to please everyone. - Bill Cosby

I don't know the key to success, but the key to failure is trying to please everybody. – Bill Cosby

I don't think meals have any business being deductible. I'm for separation of calories and corporations. - Ralph Nader

I don't think there's anything to be afraid of. Failure

brings great rewards -- in the life of an artist. - Quentin Tarantino

I don't think there's anything unique about human intelligence. All the neurons in the brain that make up perceptions and emotions operate in a binary fashion. - Bill Gates

I don't work according to nature, but in front and together with it. An artist must observe the nature, but never confuse it with the art. - Pablo Picasso

I feel sorry for short people, you know. When it rains, they're the last to know. - Rodney Dangerfield

I find that when you have a real interest in life and a curious life, that sleep is not the most important thing. - Martha Stewart

I get to go to lots of overseas places, like Canada. - Britney Spears

I get to play golf for a living. What more can you ask for - getting paid for doing what you love. - Tiger Woods

I guess the only way to stop divorce is to stop marriage. - Will Rogers

I have an intense desire to return to the womb. Anybody's. - Woody Allen

I have discovered photography. Now I can kill myself. I have nothing else to learn. - Pablo Picasso

I haven't been with a woman in nine months. - Mike Tyson

I honestly think it is better to be a failure at something you love than to be a success at something you hate. - George Burns

I know nothing about sex because I was always married. - Zsa Zsa Gabor

I like to say that I'm bisexual ... when I want sex, I buy it. - Boy George

I love mankind; it's people I can't stand. - Charles Schulz

I love sleep. My life has the tendency to fall apart when I'm awake, you know? - Ernest Hemingway

I love Thanksgiving. It's the only time in Los Angeles that you see natural breasts. - Arnold Schwarzenegger

I married the first man I ever kissed. When I tell this to my children, they just about throw up. - Barbara Bush

I never forget a face, but in your case I'll be glad to make an exception. - Groucho Marx

I saw this in a movie about a bus that had to SPEED around a city, keeping its SPEED over fifty, and if its SPEED dropped, it would explode! I think it was called, 'The Bus That Couldn't Slow Down.' - Homer Simpson

I still have my feet on the ground, I just wear better shoes. - Oprah Winfrey

I stopped getting the girl about ten years ago. Which is just as well because I'd forgotten what I wanted her for. - John Wayne

I think having land and not ruining it is the most beautiful art that anybody could ever want to own.
– Andy Warhol

I think it's the duty of the comedian to find out where the line is drawn and cross it deliberately. - George Carlin

I think your whole life shows in your face and you should be proud of that. - Lauren Bacall

I want to put a ding in the universe. - Steve Jobs

I was told to avoid the business all together because of the rejection. People would say to me, 'Don't you want to have a normal job and a normal family?' I guess that would be good advice for some people, but I wanted to act. - Jennifer Aniston

I wasn't satisfied just to earn a good living. I was looking to make a statement. - Donald Trump

I will honor Christmas in my heart, and try to keep it all the year. - Charles Dickens

I'd just as soon play tennis with the net down. - Robert Frost

Identify your problems but give your power and energy to solutions. - Tony Robbins

If God didn't want us to eat animals, why did he make them out of meat? - Homer Simpson

If he's so smart, how come he's dead? - Homer Simpson

If I have seen further, it is by standing on the
shoulders of giants. - Isaac Newton

If I should die tomorrow, I will have no regrets. I
did what I wanted to do. You can't expect more
from life. - Bruce Lee

If it looks like a duck, and quacks like a duck, we
have at least to consider the possibility that we have
a small aquatic bird of the family anatidae on our
hands. - Douglas Adams

If it weren't for Philo T. Farnsworth, inventor of television, we'd still be eating frozen radio dinners. - Johnny Carson

If I've made it a little easier for artists to work in violence, great! I've accomplished something. - Quentin Tarantino

If more of us valued food and cheer and song above hoarded gold, it would be a merrier world. - J.R.R. Tolkien

If one knows exactly what is going to be done, why do it? - Pablo Picasso

If stupidity got us into this mess, then why can't it get us out? - Will Rogers

If the career you have chosen has some unexpected inconvenience, console yourself by reflecting that no career is without them. - Jane Fonda

If there's anything unsettling to the stomach, it's watching actors on television talk about their personal lives. - Marlon Brando

If variety is the spice of life, marriage is the big can of leftover Spam. - Johnny Carson

If we don't end war, war will end us. - H.G. Wells

If you are going to achieve excellence in big things, you develop the habit in little matters. Excellence is not an exception, it is a prevailing attitude. - Colin Powell

If you are gonna kick society in the teeth, you might as well use both feet. - Keith Richards

If you can dream it, you can do it! - Walt Disney

If you get an impulse in a scene, no matter how wrong it seems, follow the impulse. It might be something and if it ain't - take two! - Jack Nicholson

If you look back on the '60s and think there was more good than harm, you're probably a Democrat. If you think there was more harm than good, you're probably a Republican. - Bill Clinton

If you want to sacrifice the admiration of many men for the criticism of one, go ahead, get married. - Katherine Hepburn

If you want to succeed you should strike out on new paths, rather than travel the worn paths of accepted success. - John Rockefeller

If you've got them by the balls, their hearts and minds will follow. - John Wayne

If you're given a choice between money and sex appeal, take the money. As you get older, the money will become your sex appeal. - Katherine Hepburn

If you're successful, acting is about as soft a job as anybody could ever wish for. But if you're unsuccessful it's worse than having a skin disease. - Marlon Brando

I'll always perform, because show business is in my blood. Or maybe it's in my feet. Wherever it is, I don't think I'll ever stop. - Robin Williams

I'm astounded by people who want to 'know' the universe when it's hard enough to find your way around Chinatown. - Woody Allen

I'm at an age where I think more about food than sex. Last week I put a mirror over my dining room table. - Rodney Dangerfield

I'm just like anyone. I cut and I bleed. And I embarrass easily. - Michael Jackson

I'm like that guy who single-handedly built the rocket & flew to the moon! What was his name? Apollo Creed? - Homer Simpson

I'm not normally a religious man, but if you're up there, save me, Superman! - Homer Simpson

I'm not upset about my divorce. I'm only upset I'm not a widow. - Roseanne Barr

I'm number 10 at the box office. Right under Barbra Streisand. Can you imagine being under Barbra Streisand? Get me a bag. I may throw up. - Walter Matthau

I'm totally at home on the stage. That's where I live. That's where I was born. That's where I'm safe. - Michael Jackson

In business, I've discovered that my purpose is to do my best to my utmost ability every day. That's my standard. I learned early in my life that I had high standards. - Donald Trump

In doubt a man of worth will trust to his own wisdom. - J.R.R. Tolkien

In order to succeed, your desire for success should be greater than your fear of failure. - Bill Cosby

In politics, strangely enough, the best way to play your cards is to lay them face upwards on the table. - H.G. Wells

Innovation distinguishes between a leader and a follower. - Steve Jobs

Innovation distinguishes between a leader and a follower. - Steve Jobs

Intellectual property has the shelf life of a banana. - Bill Gates

It does not do to dwell on dreams and forget to live. - J.K. Rowling

It doesn't matter how many people I've killed. What matters is how I get along with the people who are still alive. - Bruce Willis

It is a mistake to think you can solve any major problems just with potatoes. - Douglas Adams

It is inevitable that some defeat will enter even the most victorious life. The human spirit is never finished when it is defeated ... it is finished when it surrenders. - Ben Stein

It is not fair to ask of others what you are not willing to do yourself. - Eleanor Roosevelt

It is your work in life that is the ultimate seduction. - Pablo Picasso

It takes a long time to turn a big country around. - Bill Clinton

'It will obliterate your senses!' reports David Gillin, who obviously writes autobiographically. - Roger Ebert

It's better to be good than evil, but one achieves goodness at a terrific cost. - Stephen King

It's going to be the ballot or the bullet. - Malcolm X

It's kind of fun to do the impossible. - Walt Disney

I've been accused of vulgarity. I say that's bullshit. - Mel Brooks

I've got more trophies than Wayne Gretzky & The Pope combined! - Homer Simpson

I've had a wonderful time, but this wasn't it. - Groucho Marx

I've never learned anything while I was talking. - Larry King

I've worked for four presidents and watched two others up close, and I know that there's no such

thing as a routine day in the Oval Office. - Dick
Cheney

Jim Bakker spells his name with two k's because
three would be too obvious. - Bill Maher

Just as war is freedom's cost, disagreement is
freedom's privilege. - Bill Clinton

Just because I look sexy on the cover of Rolling
Stone doesn't mean I'm naughty. - Britney Spears

Just because something doesn't do what you planned it to do doesn't mean it's useless. - Thomas Edison

Just in terms of allocation of time resources, religion is not very efficient. There's a lot more I could be doing on a Sunday morning. - Bill Gates

Kids, just because I don't care doesn't mean I'm not listening. - Homer Simpson

Knowledge speaks, but wisdom listens. - Jimi Hendrix

Laughter and tears are both responses to frustration and exhaustion. I myself prefer to laugh, since there is less cleaning up to do afterward. - Kurt Vonnegut

Leadership is solving problems. The day soldiers stop bringing you their problems is the day you have stopped leading them. They have either lost confidence that you can help or concluded you do not care. Either case is a failure of leadership. - Colin Powell

Let us celebrate our agreement with the adding of chocolate to milk. - Homer Simpson

Let us now set forth one of the fundamental truths about marriage: the wife is in charge. - Bill Cosby

Liberty without learning is always in peril; learning without liberty is always in vain. - John F. Kennedy

Life is just one damned thing after another. - Elbert Hubbard

Life is just one grand sweet song, so start the music. - Ronald Reagan

Life is not a support system for art. It's the other way around. - Stephen King

Life is pleasant. Death is peaceful. It's the transition that's troublesome. - Jimi Hendrix

Life is what happens to you while you're busy making other plans. - John Lennon

Like everyone else who makes the mistake of getting older, I begin each day with coffee and obituaries. - Bill Cosby

Logic will get you from A to B - Imagination will take you everywhere - Albert Einstein

Look, all I'm saying is, if these big stars didn't want people going through their garbage and saying they're gay, then they shouldn't have tried to express themselves creatively. - Homer Simpson

Love is the answer, but while you are waiting for the answer, sex raises some pretty good questions. - Woody Allen

Love yourself first and everything else falls into line.
You really have to love yourself to get anything
done in this world. - Lucille Ball

Luck is not chance, it is toil. Fortune is expensive
smile is earned. - Emily Dickinson

Many interviewers when they come to talk to me,
think they're being progressive by not mentioning in
their stories any longer that I'm black. I tell them,
'Don't stop now. If I shot somebody you'd mention
it.' - Colin Powell

Many that live deserve death. And some die that
deserve life. Can you give it to them? Then be not

too eager to deal out death in the name of justice, fearing for your own safety. Even the wise cannot see all ends. - J.R.R. Tolkien

Mathematics is the language with which God has written the universe. - Galileo Galilei

Middle age is when your age starts to show around your middle. - Bob Hope

Money doesn't make you happy. I now have $50 million, but I was just as happy when I had $48 million. - Arnold Schwarzenegger

Money doesn't talk, it swears. - Bob Dylan

More than any time in history mankind faces a crossroads. One path leads to despair and utter hopelessness, the other to total extinction. Let us pray that we have the wisdom to choose correctly. - Woody Allen

Mothers all want their sons to grow up to be president, but they don't want them to become politicians in the process. - John F. Kennedy

My doctor told me to stop having intimate dinners for four. Unless there are three other people. - Orson Welles

My favorite animal is steak. - Fran Lebowitz

My goal is simple. It is a complete understanding of the universe, why it is as it is and why it exists at all. - Stephen Hawking

My grandmother started walking five miles a day when she was sixty. She's ninety-five now, and we don't know where the hell she is. - Ellen DeGeneres

My life has no purpose, no direction, no aim, no meaning, and yet I'm happy. I can't figure it out. What am I doing right? - Charles Schulz

My main objective is to be professional but to kill him. - Mike Tyson

My mother never saw the irony in calling me a son-of-a-bitch. - Jack Nicholson

My philosophy is that not only are you responsible

for your life, but doing the best at this moment puts you in the best place for the next moment. - Oprah Winfrey

Never continue in a job you don't enjoy. If you're happy in what you're doing, you'll like yourself, you'll have inner peace. And if you have that, along with physical health, you will have had more success than you could possibly have imagined. - Johnny Carson

No evil can happen to a good man, either in life or after death. – Plato

No government can love a child, and no policy can

substitute for a family's care. - Hillary Clinton

No matter how hard the loss, defeat might serve as well as victory to shake the soul and let the glory out. - Al Gore

No matter what they're charging to get in, it's worth more to get out. - Roger Ebert

No one can make you feel inferior without your consent. - Eleanor Roosevelt

No problem is so formidable that you can't walk away from it. - Charles Schulz

No, no, no, Lisa. If adults don't like their jobs, they don't go on strike. They just go in every day and do it really half-assed. - Homer Simpson

Not for nothing is their motto TGIF - 'Thank God It's Friday.' They live for the weekends, when they can go do what they really want to do. - Richard Nelson Bolles

Not only does God play dice, but he sometimes throws them where they cannot be seen. - Stephen Hawking

Nothing separates the generations more than music. By the time a child is eight or nine, he has developed a passion for his own music that is even stronger than his passions for procrastination and weird clothes. - Bill Cosby

Nothing travels faster than the speed of light, with the possible exception of bad news, which obeys its own set of laws. - Douglas Adams

Obstacles don't have to stop you. If you run into a wall, don't turn around and give up. Figure out how to climb it, go through it, or work around it. - Michael Jordan

Oh, man, what a day. It's no cakewalk being a single parent, juggling a career and family like so many juggling balls ... two, I suppose. - Chief Wiggum

Old people don't need companionship. They need to be isolated and studied so it can be determined what nutrients they have that might be extracted for our personal use. - Homer Simpson

On the plus side, death is one of the few things that can be done just as easily lying down. - Woody Allen

One thing I have learned about the presidency is that whatever shortcomings you have, people are going to notice them -- and whatever strengths you have, you're going to need them. - George W. Bush

Only one man in a thousand is a leader of men. The other 999 follow women. - Groucho Marx

Our destiny is bound up with the destiny of every other American. - Bill Clinton

Our flag is red, white and blue, but our nation is a rainbow -- red, yellow, brown, black and white -- and we're all precious in God's sight. - Jesse Jackson

Our true nationality is mankind. - H.G. Wells

Outside of a dog, a book is a man's best friend. Inside of a dog, it is too dark to read. - Groucho Marx

Over the years, the United States has sent many of its fine young men and women into great peril to fight for freedom beyond our borders. The only amount of land we have ever asked for in return is enough to bury those that did not return. - Colin Powell

Parents are not interested in justice, they're interested in peace and quiet. - Bill Cosby

People are definitely a company's greatest asset. It doesn't make any difference whether the product is cars or cosmetics. A company is only as good as the people it keeps. - Mary Kay Ash

People want to know why I do this, why I write such gross stuff. I like to tell them that I have the heart of a small boy ... and I keep it in a jar on my desk. - Stephen King

People will pay more to be entertained than educated. - Johnny Carson

Please, if you ever see me getting beaten up by the police, please put your video camera down and help me. - Bobcat Goldthwait

Political language is designed to make lies sound truthful and murder respectable, and to give an appearance of solidity to pure wind. - George Orwell

Politics has got so expensive that it takes lots of money to even get beat with. - Will Rogers

Politics is the art of looking for trouble, finding it everywhere, diagnosing it incorrectly, and applying the wrong remedies. - Groucho Marx

Power is not a means, it is an end. One does not establish a dictatorship in order to safeguard a revolution; one makes the revolution in order to establish the dictatorship. - George Orwell

Put out an APB for a male suspect, driving a... car of some sort, heading in the direction of, uh, you know, that place that sells chili. Suspect is hatless. Repeat, hatless. - Chief Wiggum

Quote me as saying I was mis-quoted. - Groucho

Marx

Real freedom is having nothing. I was freer when I didn't have a cent. – Mike Tyson

Real integrity is doing the right thing, knowing that nobody's going to know whether you did it or not. - Oprah Winfrey

Real loss is only possible when you love something more than you love yourself. - Robin Williams

Remember, if you smoke after sex you're doing it too fast. - Woody Allen

---

Sex at age ninety is like trying to shoot pool with a rope. - George Burns

---

Sex is emotion in motion. - Mae West

Sex without love is a meaningless experience, but as far as meaningless experiences go, it's pretty damn good. - Woody Allen

She didn't reckon with the awesome power of the Chief of Police! Now where did I put my badge? ... Hey, that duck's got it! - Chief Wiggum

Short-circuiting the long-established principles of patient negotiation leads to war, not peace. - Jimmy Carter

Sitting at the table doesn't make you a diner, unless you eat some of what's on that plate. Being here in America doesn't make you an American. Being born here in America doesn't make you an American. - Malcolm X

So far as I can remember, there is not one word in

the Gospels in praise of intelligence. - Bertrand
Russell

So where's the Cannes Film Festival being held this
year? - Christina Aguilera

Some men would rather pursue happiness than
obtain it. - Roger Ebert

Some national parks have long waiting lists for
camping reservations. When you have to wait a year
to sleep next to a tree, something is wrong. - George
Carlin

Someone lying back getting a wank absolutely should be something we see in cinema. - Ewan McGregor

Success is a lousy teacher. It seduces smart people into thinking they can't lose. - Bill Gates

Success is getting what you want. Happiness is wanting what you get. - Dale Carnegie

Success is liking yourself, liking what you do, and

liking how you do it. - Maya Angelou

Talent is cheaper than table salt. What separates the talented individual from the successful one is a lot of hard work. - Stephen King

Talking about music is like dancing about architecture. - Steve Martin

Television has brought back murder into the home, where it belongs. - Alfred Hitchcock

Television is where you watch people in your living room that you would not want near your house. - Groucho Marx

That's one small step for man, one giant leap for mankind. - Neil Armstrong

The average celebrity meets, in one year, ten times the amount of people that the average person meets in his entire life. - Jack Nicholson

The best minds are not in government. If any were, business would steal them away. - Ronald Reagan

The best thinking has been done in solitude. The worst has been done in turmoil.   - Thomas Edison

The Bible looks like it started out as a game of Mad Libs. - Bill Maher

The cable TV sex channels don't expand our horizons, don't make us better people and don't come in clearly enough. - Bill Maher

The cool thing about being famous is traveling. I

have always wanted to travel across seas, like to
Canada and stuff. - Britney Spears

The cost of freedom is always high, but Americans
have always paid it. And one path we shall never
choose, and that is the path of surrender, or
submission. - John F. Kennedy

The days of looking the other way while despotic
regimes trample human rights, rob their nations'
wealth, and then excuse their failings by feeding
their people a steady diet of anti-Western hatred are
over. - Dick Cheney

The difference between Los Angeles and yogurt is

that yogurt comes with less fruit. - Rush Limbaugh

The federal government has taken too much tax money from the people, too much authority from the states, and too much liberty with the Constitution. - Ronald Reagan

The first rule of any technology used in a business is that automation applied to an efficient operation will magnify the efficiency. The second is that automation applied to an inefficient operation will magnify the inefficiency. - Bill Gates

The function of leadership is to produce more leaders, not more followers. - Ralph Nader

The good people sleep much better at night than the bad people. Of course, the bad people enjoy the waking hours much more. - Woody Allen

The greatest thing you can do is surprise yourself. - Steve Martin

The heart of marriage is memories; and if the two of you happen to have the same ones and can savor your reruns, then your marriage is a gift from the gods. - Bill Cosby

The laws of gravity cannot be held responsible for people falling in love. - Albert Einstein

The miracle is not that we do this work, but that we are happy to do it. - Mother Teresa

The more sensitive you are, the more likely you are to be brutalized, develop scabs and never evolve. Never allow yourself to feel anything because you always feel too much. - Marlon Brando

The most important things are the hardest things to say. They are the things you get ashamed of because words diminish your feelings - words shrink things that seem timeless when they are in your head to no

more than living size when they are brought out. -
Stephen King

The new rage is to say that the government is the
cause of all our problems, and if only we had no
government, we'd have no problems. I can tell you,
that contradicts evidence, history, and common
sense. - Bill Clinton

The only monster here is the gambling monster that
has enslaved your mother! I call him Gamblor, and
it's time to snatch your mother from his neon claws!
- Homer Simpson

The only reason I'm in Hollywood is that I don't

have the moral courage to refuse the money. - Marlon Brando

The path to youth takes a whole life. - Pablo Picasso

The reason I love my dog so much is because when I come home, he's the only one in the world who treats me like I'm The Beatles. - Bill Maher

The secret of acting is sincerity. If you can fake that, you've got it made. -George Burns

The Social Contract is nothing more or less than a vast conspiracy of human beings to lie to and humbug themselves and one another for the general good. Lies are the mortar that bind the savage individual man into the social masonry. - H.G. Wells

The statistics on sanity are that one out of every four Americans are suffering from some form of mental illness. Think of your three best friends. If they're okay, then it's you. - Rita Mae Brown

The Supreme Court has ruled that they cannot have a nativity scene in Washington, D.C. This wasn't for any religious reasons. They couldn't find three wise men and a virgin. - Jay Leno

The survival of liberty in our land increasingly depends on the success of liberty in other lands. - George W. Bush

The thing we all have to understand to put these last two years in focus, is that liberals in this country care more about whether European leaders like us than they do about whether terrorists are killing us. - Rush Limbaugh

The trust of the innocent is the liar's most useful tool. - Stephen King

The usual approach of science of constructing a mathematical model cannot answer the questions of why there should be a universe for the model to describe. Why does the universe go to all the bother of existing? - Stephen Hawking

The White House: I don't know whether it's the finest public housing in America or the crown jewel of the prison system. - Bill Clinton

The whole history of science has been the gradual realization that events do not happen in an arbitrary manner, but that they reflect a certain underlying order, which may or may not be divinely inspired. - Stephen Hawking

The wise speak only of what they know. - J.R.R.

Tolkien

The writer's job is not to judge, but to seek to understand. - Ernest Hemingway

There are no secrets to success. It is the result of preparation, hard work, and learning from failure. - Colin Powell

There are painters who transform the sun to a yellow spot, but there are others who with the help of their art and their intelligence, transform a yellow spot into the sun. - Pablo Picasso

There are some who've forgotten why we have a military. It's not to promote war; it's to be prepared for peace. - Ronald Reagan

There are two kinds of people in this world: Michael Jackson fans and losers. - Seth Green

There cannot be true democracy unless women's voices are heard. - Hillary Clinton

There comes a time when deceit and defiance must

be seen for what they are. At that point, a gathering danger must be directly confronted. At that point, we must show that beyond our resolutions is actual resolve. -Dick Cheney

There is hope for the future because God has a sense of humor and we are funny to God. - Bill Cosby

There is no charm equal to tenderness of heart. - Jane Austen

There is no secrets to success don't waste time looking for them. Success is the result of perfection, hard work, learning from failure, loyalty to those for whom your work and persistence. - Colin Powell

There is no terror in the bang, only in the anticipation of it. - Alfred Hitchcock

There is no time for cut-and-dried monotony. There is time for work. And time for love. That leaves no other time! - Coco Chanel

There is nothing wrong with America that cannot be cured by what is right with America. - Bill Clinton

There's a difference between a philosophy and a

bumper sticker. - Charles Schulz

———— ❧ ————

Think left and think right and think low and think high. Oh, the thinks you can think up if only you try! - Theodor Seuss Geisel

———— ❧ ————

Think of all the beauty that's still left in and around you, and be happy. - Anne Frank

———— ❧ ————

This country was built on rape, slavery, murder, degradation and affiliation with crime. - Mike Tyson

———— ❧ ————

This moment contains all moments. - C.S. Lewis

Those are my principles. If you don't like them I
have others. - Groucho Marx

Time takes it all, whether you want it to or not. Time
takes it all, time bears it away, and in the end there
is only darkness. Sometimes we find others in that
darkness, and sometimes we lose them there again. -
Stephen King

To grasp the full significance of life is the actor's
duty, to interpret it is his problem and to express it
his dedication. - Marlon Brando

To write history one must be more than a man, since the author who holds the pen of this great justiciary must be free from all preoccupation of interest or vanity. - Napoleon Bonaparte

Today we can declare: Government is not the problem, and government is not the solution. We, the American people, we are the solution. - Bill Clinton

Today, you always know whether you are on the Internet or on your PC's hard drive. Tomorrow, you will not care and may not even know. - Bill Gates

Today's students can put dope in their veins or hope in their brains. If they can conceive it and believe it, they can achieve it. They must know it is not their aptitude, but their attitude, that will determine their altitude. - Jesse Jackson

Too bad the only people who know how to run the country are busy driving cabs and cutting hair. - George Burns

Too much of a good thing can be wonderful. - Mae West

Tragedy is when I cut my finger. Comedy is when you walk into an open sewer and die. - Mel Brooks

True peace is not merely the absence of tension: it is the presence of justice. - Martin Luther King Jr.

Truly wonderful, the mind of a child is. - Jedi Master Yoda

Under the doctrine of the separation of powers, the manner in which the president personally exercises his assigned executive powers is not subject to questioning by another branch of government. - Richard Nixon

Undertake not what you cannot perform, but be careful to keep your promise – Washington

Wal-Mart, what's that? Do they, like, make walls there? - Paris Hilton

War-making doesn't stop war-making. If it did, our problems would have stopped millennia ago. - Colman McCarthy

Washington is a city of Southern efficiency and Northern charm. - John F. Kennedy

Washington is a Hollywood for ugly people.
Hollywood is a Washington for the simpleminded. -
John McCain

We always overestimate the change that will occur
in the next two years and underestimate the change
that will occur in the next ten. - Bill Gates

We cannot be both the world's leading champion of
peace and the world's leading supplier of arms. -
Jimmy Carter

We have the Bill of Rights. What we need is a Bill of Responsibilities. - Bill Maher

---

We make war that we may live in peace. – Aristotle

We must never forget that art is not a form of propaganda; it is a form of truth. - John F. Kennedy

---

We need not just a new generation of leadership but a new gender of leadership. - Bill Clinton

---

We turn not older with years, but newer every day. - Emily Dickinson

Weaseling out of things is important to learn. It's what separates us from the animals ... except the weasel. - Homer Simpson

What if a kid goes to school after seeing. - Kill Bill

What IS your fascination with my forbidden closet of mysteries? - Chief Wiggum

What makes us men is that we can think logically. What makes us human is that we sometimes choose not to. - Roger Ebert

What you do speaks so loud that I cannot hear what you say. – Emerson

When asked, 'How do you write?' I invariably answer, 'one word at a time.' - Stephen King

When choosing between two evils, I always like to try the one I've never tried before. - Mae West

When I first heard that Marge was joining the police academy, I thought it would be fun and zany, like that movie Spaceballs. But instead it was dark and disturbing. Like that movie -- Police Academy. - Homer Simpson

When I got my first television set, I stopped caring so much about having close relationships. - Andy Warhol

When I took office, only high energy physicists had ever heard of what is called the Worldwide Web ... now even my cat has its own page. - Bill Clinton

When I was younger I could remember anything, whether it happened or not. - Mark Twain

When we're unemployed, we're called lazy; when the whites are unemployed it's called a depression. - Jesse Jackson

When you are good to others you are best to yourself. - Dale Carnegie

When you become senile, you won't know it. - Bill Cosby

When you stand for your liberty, we will stand with you. - George W. Bush

---

When you stop giving and offering something to the rest of the world, it's time to turn out the lights. - George Burns

---

When you're comfortable with someone you love, the silence is the best. - Britney Spears

---

Why is it that you physicists always require so

much expensive equipment? Now the Department of Mathematics requires nothing but money for paper, pencils, and erasers ... and the Department of Philosophy is better still. It doesn't even ask for erasers. - Isaac Asimov

Women need a reason to have sex -- men just need a place. - Billy Crystal

Women should be obscene and not heard.- Groucho Marx

Would people applaud me if I was a good plumber? - Marlon Brando

You can have it all. You just can't have it all at once.
- Oprah Winfrey

You can turn painful situations around through laughter. If you can find humor in anything, even poverty, you can survive it. - Bill Cosby

You can't wait for inspiration. You have to go after it with a club. - Jack London

You can't deny laughter; when it comes, it plops

down in your favorite chair and stays as long as it wants. - Stephen King

You do what you are ... You're born with a gift. If not that, then you get good at something along the way. And what you're good at. You don't take for granted. - Morgan Freeman

You gain strength, experience and confidence by every experience where you really stop to look fear in the face. You must do the thing you cannot do. - Eleanor Roosevelt

You know what your problem is? It's that you haven't seen enough movies - all of life's riddles are

answered in the movies. - Steve Martin

You know, there's a million fine looking women in the world, dude. But they don't all bring you lasagna at work. Most of 'em just cheat on you. - Kevin Smith

You may think the President is all-powerful, but he is not. He needs a lot of guidance from the Lord. - Barbara Bush

You only lie to two people in your life: your girlfriend and the police. - Jack Nicholson

You won't get anything unless you have the vision to imagine it. - John Lennon

You're most unhappy customers are your greatest source of learning. - Bill Gates

Youth has no age. - Pablo Picasso

We have always ben shameless about stealing great ideas. - Steve Jobs

ABOUT THE AUTHOR

 Growing up in a small town in India, Susheel heard a story. A child goes to a fair and sees a man selling balloons; he watches the red balloon fly away high into the sky. He asks the balloon vendor, "Will the green balloon fly into the sky as well?" The balloon man says, "Yes." Next the child asks, "How about the black balloon?" The balloon vendor replies, "It is not the color of the balloon, but what is in it that takes the balloon high into the sky."

Susheel has lived with a strong belief that "it is what you have in you that takes you the places you want to go, it does not matter where you come from, all that matters is where you are going."

Susheel has a passion for quotes, sayings, and studying interesting facts about history and their relevance in the modern world. In the past decade, he has consulted with fortune 500 clients advising them on business strategies.